This book be

_____

©Tabitha Barnett 2016 www.facebook.com/tabbystangledart

©Tabitha Barnett 2016   www.facebook.com/tabbystangledart

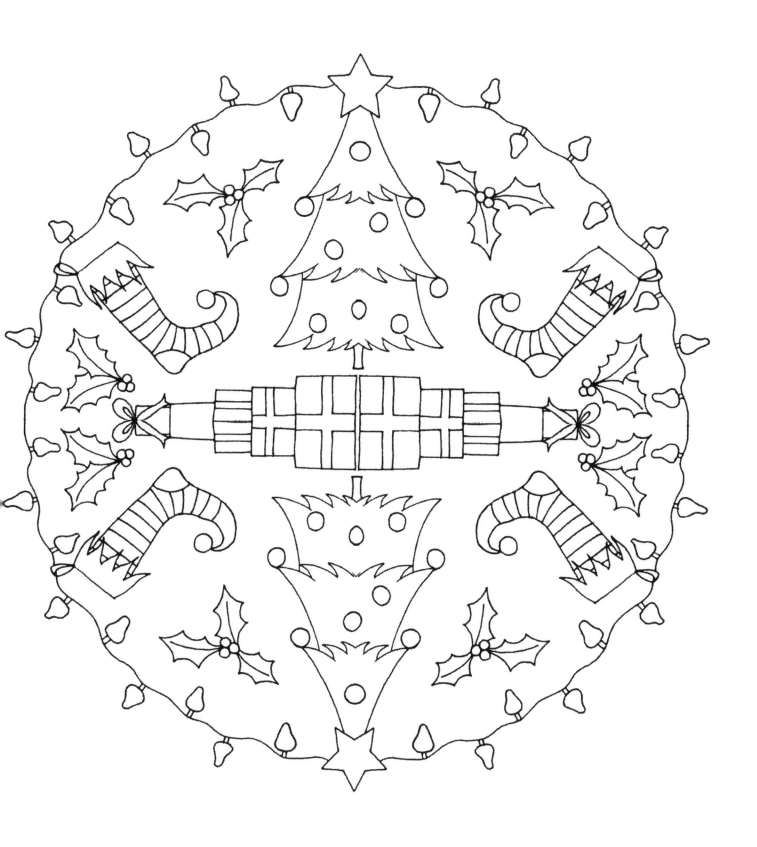

©Tabitha Barnett 2016 www.facebook.com/tabbystangledart

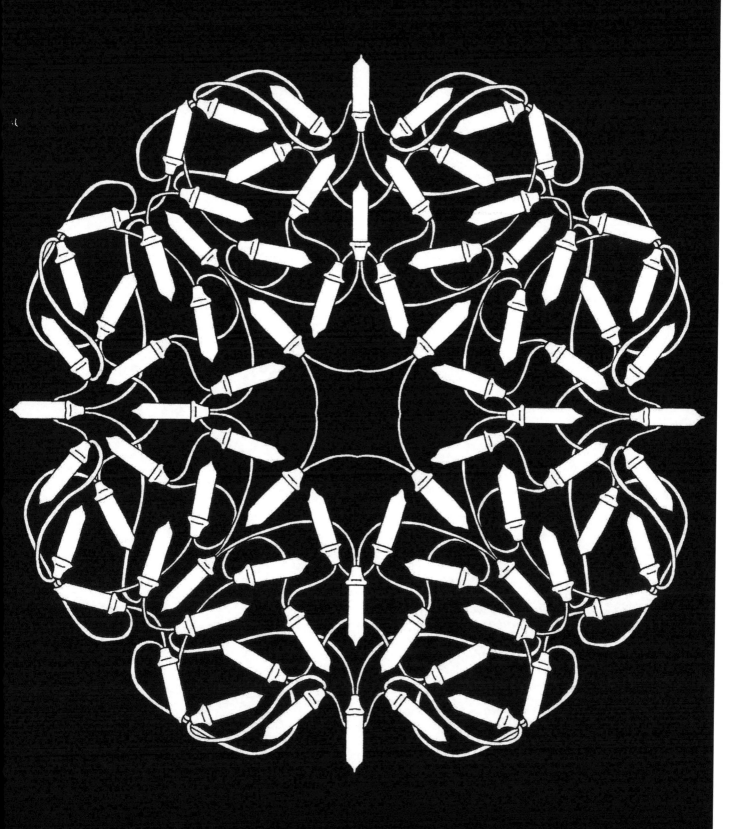

©Tabitha Barnett 2016   www.facebok.com/tabbystangledart

©Tabitha Barnett 2016   www.facebook.com/tabbystangledart

©Tabitha Barnett 2016　　　www.facebook.com/tabbystangledart

©Tabitha Barnett 2016   www.facebook.com/tabbystangledart

©Tabitha Barnett 2016   www.facebook.com/tabbystangledart

©Tabitha Barnett 2016 www.facebook.com/tabbystangledart

©Tabitha Barnett 2016 www.facebook.com/tabbystangledart

MERRY CHRISTMAS

©Tabitha Barnett 2015

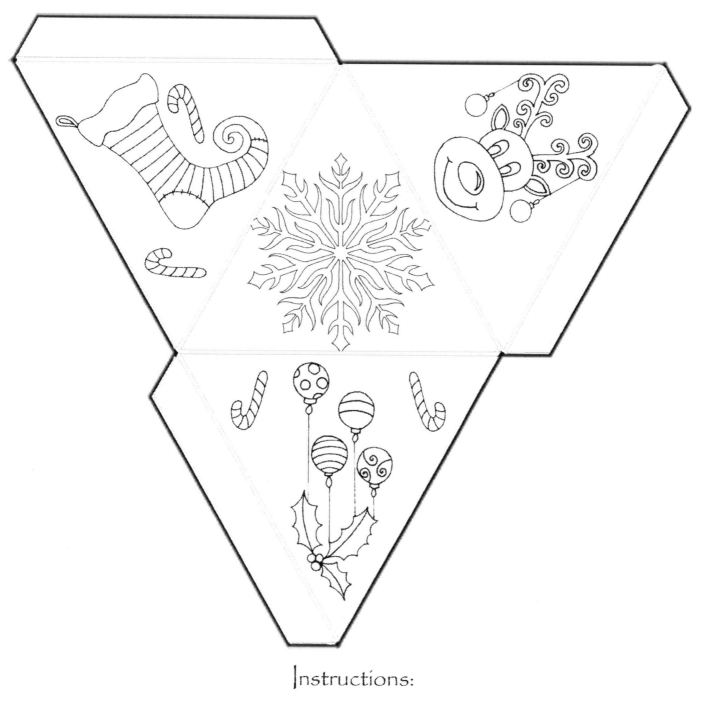

Instructions:

1. COLOR the designs.
2. CUT out design along the dark black lines.
3. FOLD along the thin double lines.
4. TAPE string or ribbon on the inside top of one of the triangles.
5. GLUE flaps to under sides and allow to dry.
6. HANG!

Instructions:

1. COLOR the designs.
2. CUT out design along the solid lines.
3. FOLD along the dotted lines.
4. TAPE string or ribbon on the inside top of one of the triangles.
5. GLUE flaps to under sides and allow to dry.

©Tabitha Barnett 2016

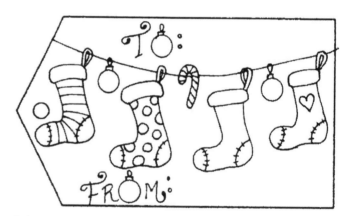

www.facebook.com/tabbystangledart

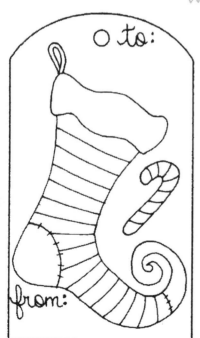

©Tabitha Barnett 2016

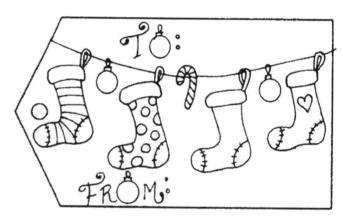

www.facebook.com/tabbystangledart

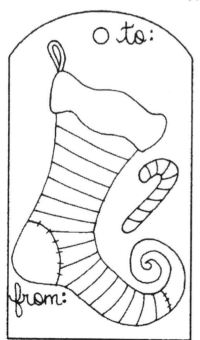

All images ©Tabitha Barnett/Tabby's Tangled Art 2016. All rights reserved. For personal use only. Do not post uncolored images online. Reproduction for PERSONAL USE ONLY is acceptable. Please DO, share your colored pages with us! #tabbbystangledart or #tabithabarnett when you share so that I can find them!

Thank You for your purchase! You cand find all of my books in both PDF and Paperback formats here:

www.amazon.com/author/tabbystangledart

www.sellfy.com/tabbyb

Become a patron for as little as $1 per month to get new fresh coloring pages in your inbox every month!

Www.patreon.com/tabbyb

Add me on facebook and like my artist page to stay up to date and get free printables!

Www.facebook.com/tabbystangledart

Join my coloring group on facebook:

https://www.facebook.com/groups/758530534289750/

Follow me on twitter:

@tabbyleann

Get some awesome colorable merchandise like tote bags, greeting cards, notebooks and more:

www.redbubble.com/people/tabbyb

Email: tabbystangledart@gmail.com

Did you enjoy this book? Please leave a review on Amazon. I love to hear from you! If you own any of my books, reviews on Amazon are ALWAYS GREATLY APPRECIATED! Amazon reviews are one of the easiestways to help indy artists like myself.

Made in the USA
Middletown, DE
09 November 2018